toys and games

around the world

Godfrey Hall

Wayland

Titles in this series:

Clothes Around the World
Festivals Around the World
Food Around the World
Houses Around the World
Musical Instruments Around the World
Shops and Markets Around the World
Toys and Games Around the World
Transport Around the World

Cover pictures: Children playing marbles. Playing bat and ball on a Sri Lankan beach. Indonesian puppets. A wood-carver at work in Mexico.
Contents page: Inuit girl playing with toy sledge, Baffin Island, Canada.

Book editor: Alison Cooper
Series editor: Deb Elliott
Book design: Malcolm Walker
Cover design: Simon Balley

First published in 1995 by
Wayland (Publishers) Limited
61 Western Road, Hove
East Sussex BN3 1JD

British Library Cataloguing in Publication Data
Hall, Godfrey
Toys and Games Around the World. – (Around the World series)
I. Title II. Series
688.72

ISBN 0 7502 1563 1

Typeset by Kudos Design Services
Printed and bound by Rotolito Lombarda S.p.A., Italy

Acknowledgements
The publishers would like to thank the following for allowing their photographs to be reproduced in this book: Bryan and Cherry Alexander *contents page*, 6 (bottom), 15 (top); J Allan Cash 4, 7, 17 (top), 22; Chapel Studios 24 (top, John Heinrich); Greg Evans International Photo Library 17 (bottom, Greg Evans); Eye Ubiquitous *cover* (top right, Paul Seheult; bottom right, James Davis Travel Photography), 6 (top, Julia Waterlow), 8 (Antony Fisher), 12 (James Davis Travel Photography), 13 (Dorothy Burrows), 15 (bottom, James Davis Travel Photography), 23 (bottom, Bruce Adams), 26 (Tim Page); Chris Fairclough 27; Sally and Richard Greenhill 16; Japan Information and Cultural Centre 21; Robert Opie 10 (top); Panos Pictures 9 (Trygve Bolstad), 24 (bottom, Neil Cooper), 25 (Liba Taylor), 28 (Jon Spaull); Tony Stone Images *cover* (bottom left, David Hiser), 5 (bottom, David Hiser), 14 (Peter Cade), 19 (Ron Sutherland); Wayland Picture Library 10 (bottom, APM Studios), 11 (APM Studios), 18 (APM Studios), 20 (Reflections Photo Library), 23 (top, APM Studios); Zefa *cover* (top left), 5 (top), 29.

Contents

Toys and games

Children have always enjoyed playing with toys and games. Spinning tops like these have been around for hundreds of years. Tops are still fun to play with today.

You don't need any equipment to play chasing games, singing games and clapping games. There are other games you can play with stones, or some shells, or just a few marbles.

Toys and games can be made from all sorts of material. These animals have been carved out of wood and painted in bright colours.

Simple toys

These Egyptian children are playing with a hoop made out of a bicycle tyre.

This Inuit child is playing with a toy sledge on Baffin Island. The sledge has been made from bits of wood.

Bits of wood have also been used to make these stilts.

Moving toys

There are lots of different ways to make toys move. This tractor uses pedal power.

This boy has made his truck out of wire. It can be pushed or pulled along.

Mechanical toys

Old clockwork toys were often made of tin. To make the car work you turn the blue handle as far as you can and the car moves when you let go.

You can make some toys move without even touching them! A special handset is used to control this truck. It sends signals to the truck.

Many toys contain microchips. These are programmed to make the toy move and talk. Some dolls can cry, drink from a bottle and even wet their nappy.

Puppets

You can use strings or rods to make a puppet's legs and arms move. These beautiful puppets have been made by Indonesians.

Some puppets are glove puppets. You put your hand inside the glove and move your fingers to make it move. Mr Punch is a famous glove puppet.

Dolls

Dolls that can be dressed in different clothes are fun to play with. Thousands of dolls like these are sold every year. You can buy lots of outfits, so it can get very expensive!

This girl lives in Siberia, where it is very cold. She has dressed her doll in animal fur, to keep it warm.

These Mexican dolls have been knitted from brightly coloured wool.

Games all around

Sometimes you can play with things you find around you. You only need a few pebbles to play a game of 'jacks'.

Sand is fun to play with. You can dig holes in it, build a castle with it, or just let it run through your fingers. These children in Thailand are building a sand castle.

Snow is good for building a snowman – or for making snowballs!

Fruit games

You can play games with fruits and seeds.

In autumn, children in some countries collect conkers. Conkers are the fruits of the horse-chestnut tree. The conkers are threaded on to string. Two children try to break each other's conker or knock it off the string.

You can pretend to tell the time with a dandelion 'clock'. You blow the seeds until they have all gone. If you have to blow three times, it is 'three o'clock'.

Name the game

Some games are played all over the world, but they have different names. This playground game is called ‘hopscotch’ in Britain. In Germany it is called ‘Tempelhupfen’ and in Libya it is called ‘Neggeza’.

Another popular game is 'Paper, scissors, stone'. In Japan this game is called 'Jan-ken-pon'. Some Native Americans called it 'Tillikum'.

Singing games

These children in Uzbekistan are playing a circle game. They are singing as they dance around. Children in Britain play a circle game called ‘Ring a ring o’roses’.

Clapping games often have songs with them too. You have to remember the clapping pattern as you sing, and the song gets faster and faster.

There are lots of rhymes you can sing when you are playing with a skipping rope.

Board games

One of the oldest games is Snakes and Ladders. It is based on a very old religious game played in India.

A game called mancala is played in Asia and Africa. It can be played with just a few seeds or stones and a row of holes in the ground. Each player has to collect as many of the other players' seeds as he can, and take over their holes.

Mah Jong is often played in Asia. Long ago, it was played with cards, but when boatmen played it their cards kept blowing into the river. They made bamboo tiles to play with instead. Today the tiles are usually made of plastic.

Bat and ball games

All over Asia, children love to play cricket. They play in the street, or in any open space.

These Australian children have made some posts out of old cans and are playing a game of rounders. You try to hit the ball with the bat, and run round as many posts as you can before the ball gets back to the bowler.

Computer games

All over the world, people enjoy playing with computer games. Some games are very complicated and you often have to react very quickly to play them. In adventure games you have to solve problems and puzzles.

This girl is using the keyboard to play a game. She is being very careful to press the right keys!

Glossary

bamboo A tall kind of grass, with woody stems. The stems are used to make furniture and poles.
bowler The person who throws, or bowls, the ball for someone else to hit.
equipment Things you need to play a game, such as bats and balls, or dice and counters for a board game.
keyboard A board with raised buttons, or keys, which have letters and numbers on them. You can change things on the computer screen by pressing the keys.
marbles Small balls made of stone or glass.
mechanical Worked by a machine.
microchip A tiny part in a machine which stores information and tells the machine how to work.

Books to read

Making Toys That Move by Gillian Chapman and Pam Robson (Simon & Schuster, 1994)
My Book About Toys by Wayne Jackman (Wayland, 1991)
101 Science Tricks series (*On Paper, On Looking, On The Move*) by Roy Richards (Simon & Schuster, 1990)
Toys (*History from Objects* series) by Karen Bryant-Mole (Wayland, 1994)

More information

Would you like to find out more about the people and places you have seen in the photographs in this book? If so, read on.

pages 4–5
Children playing with home-made spinning tops in Manila in the Philippines. Spinning tops are very popular in south-east Asia.
Marbles have been played with for hundreds of years – the Roman emperor Augustus is known to have played with them in the first century BC. The aim of most games is to hit an opponent's marble.
Wood-carver at work in Mexico.

pages 6–7
Hoops made from bicycle tyres are popular throughout Africa and Asia. These children are playing at the Farafra Oasis in Egypt.
Inuit girl playing with toy sledge on Baffin Island in Canada.
Boy on stilts, Sri Lanka

pages 8–9
Boy at a play centre in Nottinghamshire, Britain.
Boy with home-made wire truck, Zambia.

pages 10–11
Clockwork car, probably made in Germany about seventy years ago.
Truck operated by remote-control.
Girl with doll containing microchip.

pages 12–13
Puppets made in Indonesia. Indonesians are famous for making beautiful puppets, especially shadow puppets.
The Punch and Judy show is a traditional part of a seaside holiday in Britain. Mr Punch has been around for a very long time – he first appeared in Italy almost 500 years ago.

pages 14–15
Nenet girl with her doll in Siberia, Russia.
Mexican dolls in national costume outside souvenir shop.

pages 16–17
Boys playing jacks in the street in China.
Children playing on the beach in Thailand.

pages 18–19
Child with a conker, the fruit of the horse-chestnut tree.
Conkers are a traditional playground game in Britain

pages 20–21
Children playing hopscotch in Britain.
'Paper, scissors, stone' is played with two people, who, at the same time, make a sign with their hands representing paper, scissors or stone. If one person has made the sign for paper and the other has made the sign for scissors, the scissors win, because scissors can cut paper. The winner is always the one who has made a sign that can damage his or her opponent.

pages 22–3
Children playing a circle game at their nursery school in Uzbekistan in the former Soviet Union.
Girls playing with a skipping rope at Anse La Raye, St Lucia, in the Caribbean.

pages 24–5
The ancient Indian version of Snakes and Ladders was known as Moksha-Patamu.
The picture shows a variation of traditional mancala, which is played in slightly different forms all over Asia and Africa. These players are in Kenya.
Mah Jong players in China.

pages 26–7
Children playing cricket in a paddy field near Kandy in Sri Lanka.
Aboriginal children at Camp Minyerri, in Northern Territory, Australia.

pages 28–9
Vienamese girl playing hand-held computer game in Hanoi.

Index